Chill with Mozart

7 tranquil masterpieces for piano

FABER ƒƒ MUSIC

Chill with
Mozart

CD track listing

1. **Serenade No.10 in B flat 'Gran Partita', K.361: Adagio** (6:01)
   German Wind Soloists

2. **Vesperae solennes de confessore, K.339: Laudate Dominum** (4:59)
   Priti Coles (Soprano), Košice Teachers' Choir

3. **Piano Concerto No.19 in F, K.459: Allegro** (12:20)
   Jenõ Jandó (piano), Concentus Hungaricus, Mátyás Antal

4. **Flute Quartet in A, K.298: Andante** (5:47)
   Jean Claud Gérard (flute), Ensemble Villa Musica

5. **String Quintet in D, K.593: Larghetto – Allegro** (9:47)
   Éder Quartet, János Fehérvári (viola)

6. **Requiem, K.626: Benedictus** (5:44)
   Magdeléna Hajóssyová, Jaroslava Horská, Josef Kundlák, Peter Mikuláš, Slovak
   Philharmonic Orchestra and Chorus, Zdenek Košler

7. **Ave Verum Corpus, K.618** (2:54)
   Košice Teachers' Choir, Johannes Wildner

8. **Serenade No.4 in D, K.203: Andante** (5:31)
   Salzburg Chamber Orchestra, Harald Nerat

9. **Concerto in C for Flute & Harp, K.299: Andantino** (7:36)
   Jiri Válek (flute), Hana Müllerová (harp), Capella Istropolitana, Richard Edlinger

10. **Sinfonia Concertante in E flat K.297b: Andantino con Variazioni** (9:00)
    Capella Istropolitana, Richard Edlinger

11. **Così fan tutte: Soave sia il vento** (3:13)
    Capella Istropolitana, Richard Edlinger

© 2006 by Faber Music Ltd
First published in 2006 by Faber Music Ltd
3 Queen Square London WC1N 3AU
Printed in England by Caligraving Ltd
Photography: www.richardduckett.com
All rights reserved.

ISBN 0-571-52436-2

To buy Faber Music publications or to find out about the full range of titles available
please contact your local music retailer or Faber Music sales enquiries.

Faber Music Limited, Burnt Mill, Elizabeth Way, Harlow, CM20 2HX England
Tel: +44 (0)1279 82 89 82   Fax: +44 (0)1279 82 89 83
sales@fabermusic.com   fabermusic.com

Introduction

Probably the greatest genius in Western musical history, Wolfgang Amadeus Mozart was born in Salzburg in 1756, the youngest child and only surviving son of Leopold Mozart. He showed early precocity both as a keyboard-player and violinist, and soon turned his hand to composition. His obvious gifts were developed under his father's tutelage, and through the patronage of the Archbishop of Salzburg the family were able to travel abroad to Paris and to London, to show off the young Mozart's remarkable gifts. A series of other journeys followed, with important operatic commissions in Italy between 1771 and 1773.

The following period proved disappointing to both father and son, as the young Mozart grew to manhood, irked by the lack of opportunity and lack of appreciation of his gifts in Salzburg where a new Archbishop proved less sympathetic. Visits to Munich, Mannheim and Paris in 1777 and 1778 brought no substantial offer of other employment and by early 1779 Mozart was reinstated in Salzburg, now as court organist.

In 1781, Mozart broke his ties with Salzburg and spent the last ten years of his life in precarious independence in Vienna, his material situation not improved by an unsuitable marriage. Initial success with German and then Italian opera and a series of subscription concerts were followed by financial difficulties. Then, in late November of 1791, Mozart became seriously ill and died in the small hours of 5th December.

Mozart's compositions were catalogued in the 19th century by Köchel, and they are now distinguished by K. numbering rather than opus numbers.

'Listening to beautiful music is one of life's great pleasures, and there's certainly no better way to relax than to the sound of dreamy works by a composer like Mozart. But after you've listened, what better than to actually get to grips with the music yourself? I know that the piano music in this book – music that reflects the chill out mood of the CD – is exactly the kind I've enjoyed playing all my life. Gorgeous pieces you can really lose yourself in; some quite challenging but none too fiendishly difficult to master. A wonderful way to chill out – and extend your repertoire while you're at it.'

Katie Derham
Classic FM presenter and ITV news presenter

Allegro

from Sonata in C (K.545)

Minuet in D

(K.355)

Andante cantabile

from Sonata in C (K.330)

Adagio in B minor

(K.540)

Andante

from Sonata in G (K.283)

Adagio

from Sonata in D (K.576)

Fantasia in D minor

(K.397)

For more in a chilled mood
try the rest of the series ...
each with a free Naxos CD

Adagio Chillout
Favourite slow movements and contemplative pieces,
including Beethoven's *Moonlight Sonata*,
Schumann's *Träumerei* and Mendelssohn's
Song without words 'Sweet Remembrance'.

0-571-52435-4

Chill with Debussy
Unmissable favourites such as *Clair de lune*,
La fille aux cheveux de lin and *Arabesque* No.1.

0-571-52437-0

Chill with Chopin
Including masterpieces such as the *'Raindrop'* Prelude,
the *March Funèbre* from Sonata in B flat minor, and
the Waltz in A flat *'L'Adieu'*.

0-571-52438-9

The Scary Sn

Written by Kyle Derby Pratt
Illustrated by Lauren Scott

AuthorHouse™
1663 Liberty Drive
Bloomington, IN 47403
www.authorhouse.com
Phone: 1 (800) 839-8640

Published by AuthorHouse 03/06/2018

ISBN: 978-1-5246-9358-9 (sc)
ISBN: 978-1-5246-9357-2 (e)

Library of Congress Control Number: 2017916131

Printed in the USA.

This book is printed on acid-free paper.

authorHOUSE®

The SCARY SNOW Day

When Timmy woke up
there was lots of snow.
Was there school today?
He did not know.

The radio was on, Timmy waited and listened. He looked out the window and the snow really glistened!

3

The DJ started talking and the news he'd just heard, made Timmy so happy, he flapped like a bird.

4

No school today, hooray! No school for us! No homework, no teachers, no riding the bus!

Timmy was so happy, he jumped and he danced. He just couldn't believe it! This was his chance!

He'd seen a huge hill down the road from his house. It was so big and so huge, he felt like a mouse.

Am I brave enough?

Compared to that hill, he was so short and so small; was he brave enough to go? He wasn't sure at all.

To slide down that hill was scary to him. He was nervous to go, the outlook was grim.

But he has to be brave. His fears he must face. He's going to do it, today of all days.

So he got bundled up in his blue and red snowsuit.....can't forget the gloves and can't forget the boots.

Timmy's ready to go. All he needs is his sled, his scarf 'round his neck and hat on his head.

Out the door and down the road as fast as a flash. Thinking of the hill and hoping he won't crash!

The closer he got to approaching the hill, his tummy started twitching, and it wouldn't keep still.

Standing at the top getting ready to go. Waiting his turn to sled in the snow.

He goes to the top and starts to sit down. Excitement and fear in his tummy turn 'round.

Sitting on the sled getting ready to go, he gives a big push and flies through the snow!

He twists and he turns. He goes side to side. What great fun, this snow sled ride!

He gets to the bottom, swishing to a stop. Smiling great big, he climbs back to the top.

He goes down again, time after time. He's conquered his fear and that's the last rhyme.

The story is over, it's come to an end. Please don't be sad, you can read it again!

The moral of the story is this:
Don't be afraid to face your fears, for we
ALL have them throughout our years.